Passionate About Pierogies

Delicious Homemade Pierogi Recipes

Kathy E. Gary

Passionate About Pierogies

Delicious Homemade Pierogi Recipes

Dedication

This book is dedicated to my grandmother who was affectionately known as Grandma Irene. She made the best pierogies ever! Her constant dedication to her family is her greatest legacy.

If you enjoy this cookbook, please pick up a FREE copy of my ebook: **Healthy Changes to Famous Desserts** (send to you via an electronic download) at:

http://tinyurl.com/HealthyDesserts

Other books by Kathy Gary

**Going Donuts for Paczki:
Easy and Delicious Family Recipes**

**Brunching on Bialys, Blini and Blintzes:
Delicious and Easy Recipes**

Table of Contents

Introduction

Welcome to **Passionate About Pierogies: Delicious Homemade Pierogi Recipes**

This book is a true labor of love. My great-grandmother came to America from Poland in the late 1800s. She brought with her a love for cooking that has been passed down through 5 generations. I have had many friends ask me for various recipes over the years and so I have decided to put them down into book form. I hope to create several volumes of recipes that I have come to love over the years. So let's get started!

To get the most out of this book, it is important to know how it is arranged.

In the first chapter of this book is The Origins of the Pierogi. Next are Tips for Making Perfect Pierogies. Take time to read this prior to making the pierogies, as it may save you both time and frustration.

One of the great things about making pierogies is that you really do not need any special tools, other than a good rolling pin. However, there are tools available to make it easier and more fun to make pierogies and Chapter 3 will talk about these. Great memories have been made with my children and grandchildren making pierogies and some of the tools available add to the magic.

To make pierogies, you need the dough and the filling. Chapter 4 is How to Make the Dough. There are several variations on dough; you may want to try them all to discover your favorite.

Chapter 5 contains recipes for the filling for the pierogi. You may be surprised by the variety. Based on your taste and need (main course, side course or dessert), there are many different types of pierogies that you can make.

Putting It Together, Chapter 6, discusses how to create the pierogi by putting the filling and the dough together.

Finally, for all of us who love pierogies but may not have the time to make each perogi individually, is Chapter 7, which describes pierogi casseroles. Same great taste, in a simpler form!

If you aren't yet Passionate About Pierogies, I hope this book changes that! And if you are, I hope this book fires up that passion!

Happy Cooking!

~ Kathy

A Little Bit of Information About Pierogies

I was introduced to the wonderful world of pierogies by my grandmother when I was a child. But pierogies have been around for centuries. Some believe that they were first created by the Chinese, while others believe their origin was in Eastern Europe.

Pierogies are usually in the shape of a half-circle or crescent, but in some cuisines they are rectangular or triangular. Pierogies are similar to the Italian ravioli and the Chinese dumpling. In Poland, where my grandparents are from, they were traditionally considered a peasant food, but over time they have become popular with everyone. In the United States, it is common to see them served at festivals, weddings and family gatherings as a cultural dish.

Pierogies are made of unleavened dough and then boiled before cooking. Typically they are deep fried, although in more recent times, they are simply fried in butter. For an interesting variation in texture, they can also be baked.

Depending on the type of filling used, they are often topped with butter, bacon, sour cream and/or onions. Our family really enjoys prune pierogies topped with whipped cream!

The most common types of pierogies are potato, cheese and mushroom. However, the possibilities are really only limited by your imagination. In this book you will find recipes for pierogi filled with meat, potatoes, cheese, onions, cabbage, sauerkraut, and prunes. One of the things I like most about pierogies is that it is not possible to get bored with this fabulous dish.

Tips for Making Perfect Pierogies

1.   If you have never made pierogies before, you may wish to follow the recipes in this book closely. With time and experience you will be able to experiment to find out what works best for you. I know you will come to enjoy creating delicious variations.

2.   I will present several different recipes for the pierogi dough. You may have your own dough recipe that you are fond of. Many cooks use a standard noodle recipe which includes eggs. Traditionally, pierogi dough does not contain eggs. I have found that by adding eggs to the pierogi dough the effect can be a more rough dough. Choosing not to add eggs will result in a more delicate pierogi, with the taste of the filling being more robust.

3.   After making the pierogies you will be boiling them in water. To keep them from sticking together, boil them in small batches with a just a touch of oil.

4.   For some of the heavier fillings, it is possible that the pierogies will split upon boiling. To avoid this, freeze the pierogies first.

5.   To make your pierogies look especially fancy, you can "ruffle" the edges. To do this, seal the edges as usual, and then starting at one end press the edge with your thumb and first finger, move a fraction and repeat, until you reach the end.

6. There are pierogi cutters, but if you do not have one, you can use a round cookie cutter or even a glass or cup placed upside down on the dough. Remember to flour the rim so that it does not stick to the dough.

Tools for Making Pierogies

As mentioned previously, the only tool needed for making pierogies is a good rolling pin. To cut out the needed round shape from the rolled out dough, you can easily use a glass turned upside down. However, there are tools available to make pierogi-making easier and more fun. If you have never made pierogies before, I would suggest making them without the tools first to see if they are a dish that you enjoy. If so, then you may want to invest in some of the tools mentioned.

The Pierogi Maker: A search on the internet for the term 'pierogi maker' will quickly yield several. One of the best that I have used is from Kuchenprofi. With this product, you can lay a piece of the rolled-out dough over the Kuchenprofi maker, add a teaspoon of filling, then flip up one side to cut, seal and crimp the edges. It creates the perfect pierogi every time in just a matter of seconds. These makers come in various sizes, from standard to half-size.

A Cookie Spoon: For those who want the perfect amount of filling every time, a cookie spoon can be helpful. I have found this to be more important when you have young children assisting you. It is easy for them to use the cookie spoon, and the pierogies always have the right amount of filling!

Rolling Pin: There are so many rolling pins available. This is an item that should be bought based on personal preference. There are rolling pins without handles, which you roll using your hands. There are marble rolling pins. There are wood rolling pins. Personally I like the marble rolling pin for rolling out pierogi dough. It is heavy and makes the job much easier. I have also found that dough is less likely to stick to the marble (sprinkled with flour) than to the wood (sprinkled with flour).

Recipes for the Pierogi Dough

There are many recipes for pierogi dough. Below are the recipes that I have had best luck with in terms of taste and texture. Although I am starting with the dough recipes for ease of reading through this cookbook, I usually make the filling first and set it aside. In this way, when I make the dough, I can make it, roll it out, cut it out and then be all ready to add the filling.

All dough recipes make between 15 – 20 pierogies.

Original Pierogi Dough

This dough recipe, without egg, will result in a lighter and smoother pocket for the pierogi filling. It takes a little more time to make, but the results are definitely worth it!

Ingredients
- 3 cups flour
- 3/4 cup boiling water
- 1/4 cup cold water
- 1/2 teaspoon salt
- 1/2 teaspoon oil

Directions

Sift flour into a bowl and add salt. Slowly add the boiling water while stirring. Use a spoon or fork to crumble up any lumps in the flour. Cover the bowl with a towel and let sit for 5 minutes.

Pour a little at a time of the cold water into the mixture, again crumbling up any of the lumps with a fork or spoon until smooth. Cover the bowl again with a towel and set aside for 10 minutes.

Add the oil and knead the dough until it's smooth.

Just a Touch of Sour Cream

Tip: This dough is especially tasty with the potato filling.

Ingredients
- 3 eggs
- 1 (8 ounce) container sour cream
- 3 cups all-purpose flour
- 1/4 teaspoon salt
- 1 tablespoon baking powder

Directions

Begin by beating together the eggs and sour cream until smooth. This can be done by hand using a spoon or with a mixer on low speed. Using a sifter, sift the flour, salt and baking powder together into the egg and sour cream mixture. Knead until dough is smooth.

A Splash of Milk

Ingredients
- 1 egg
- 1/4 cup milk
- 1/2 cup water
- 1/2 tsp. salt
- 2 cups sifted flour

Directions
In a medium sized bowl, beat egg, milk, water and salt together. This can be done by hand with a spoon or with a mixer on low speed. By hand with a spoon, slowly add flour, 1 cup at a time, until fully blended.

Standard Noodle-type Dough

Ingredients
- 2 cups all-purpose flour
- 1 teaspoon salt
- 1 egg, beaten
- 2/3 cup cold water

Directions
Mix together the flour, salt, egg and water into a bowl.
Kneed the mixture into a ball.

Rolling Out the Dough

Tip: If the dough is sticky you can add a little more flour or place it in the refrigerator for an hour or more. For best results, use a heavy rolling pin to roll out the dough.

Lightly flour your working surface and knead the dough until firm and smooth. Take enough dough to work with, about one-third to one half of the dough, and roll it out. Depending on your thickness preference (I prefer a thinner pierogi dough, so I roll it out to about 1/8 inch thickness, but you may prefer it a little thicker or thinner. Thinner pierogies will be more fragile, so handle them with care so they do not rip or split).

Cut out the dough into 3-inch rounds using a pierogi cutter, a biscuit cutter or an upside down glass (see Tip 5 in the Tips Section above).

Continue to roll out and cut dough into circles until there is no dough left.

Tip: With any left over dough, roll it out to a 1/4-inch thickness and slice it into 4 to 5 inch strips. Boil the strips in water with a teaspoon of oil, and when they begin to float, with a spoon or tongs, carefully take them out and place them in a bowl to cool. Instant, homemade noodles! These noodles are especially good in chicken noodle soup.

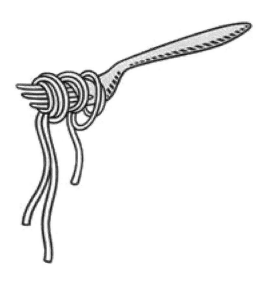

Pierogi Filling Recipes

There are many different pierogi fillings that you can make. What you choose can be determined by personal preference or entrée type. If you want to serve the pierogies as a main dish, you may want to choose a meat filling. As a side dish, the potato, cheese or onion recipe would be a good choice. For a sweet side or dessert, you can use a fruit or sweet cheese filling.

Ground Meat Filling

The ground meat filling is an excellent choice if making the pierogies as a main dish. The flavor can be enhanced by adding your favorite spices while cooking the meat. You can also top the pierogies with sautéed onions and mushrooms.

Ingredients
- 1 lb. ground beef
- 1 onion, chopped
- 1 tbsp. butter
- 1 tbsp. flour
- 1/2 tsp. dill
- salt, pepper to taste

Directions

Prepare the meat filling as follows. In a large skillet, on medium heat, sauté the chopped onion in butter. Do this lightly, for only a minute or two. Add the ground beef and sauté on medium-high heat until brown. Add salt and pepper. When meat is fully cooked, drain off any fat.

Slowly stir in the flour and dill. While still warm (but not hot) put a half-tablespoon of the meat mixture within the circle of dough.

Sauerkraut Filling

The sauerkraut filling is a favorite straight from Poland! Our family makes these pierogies for holidays and family gatherings. They are especially good on a cold winter day!

Ingredients

- 2 cups sauerkraut (rinsed)
- 2 tsp. butter
- 1 small onion, chopped
- salt, pepper to taste

Directions

Place the sauerkraut in a small pan and cook on medium-low heat in a little water. Drain. Chop the sauerkraut into small pieces. In a frying pan, sauté the onion in the butter. Add the sauerkraut to the onion and simmer for 5 minutes. Let this cool before spooning it on to the pierogi dough.

Mushroom and Onion Filling

Ingredients

- 1 cup mushrooms, chopped
- 1 onion, finely chopped
- 2 egg yolks
- 1 tablespoon butter
- salt, pepper to taste

Directions

In a small frying pan, sauté on low heat, the onion in butter. Add the mushrooms, salt and pepper and continue to sauté. Cover and simmer on low heat for 5 to 7 minutes. Remove the pan from the heat and allow the mixture to cool. Place the mixture into a bowl. Add egg yolks, stirring well. Cool completely before spooning the filling on to the dough.

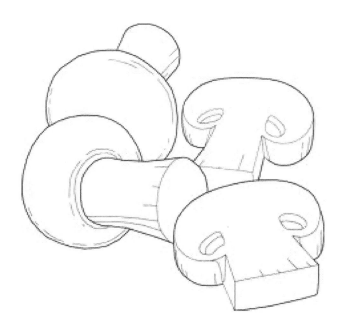

Savory Sauerkraut and Mushroom

This recipe is a family favorite. Its robust flavor is perfect on a snowy evening!

Ingredients
- 1 cup mushrooms, chopped into small pieces
- 2 cups sauerkraut
- 1 small onion, chopped finely
- butter
- salt, pepper to taste

Directions
In a small frying pan, cook the sauerkraut in a little water, on low heat for 10 minutes. Drain the sauerkraut then cut into small pieces with a knife.

In a separate frying pan, sauté the onion and mushrooms in butter. Add the sauerkraut to the onion and mushroom mixture and fry on low heat for 5 minutes. Cool completely before using filling.

Kickin' Cabbage Filling

Ingredients
- 1 small head of cabbage
- 2 cups of water
- 1 small onion, chopped
- 2 tablespoons butter
- dash of salt and pepper
- mushrooms (optional)

Directions

Shred the cabbage and place in a small pot. Cover the cabbage with enough water to cover (about one cup). Heat on high heat for about 4 minutes. Drain the cabbage. Cover the cabbage again with water (again about one cup) heat to boiling and then simmer for 20 minutes.

In a frying pan, sauté 1 chopped onion in 3 tablespoons of butter until soft and light brown in color. Stir in cabbage and add salt and pepper. Simmer, covered, until soft. Uncover and continue to cook over low heat until no more moisture is left (about 3 minutes).

Put the mixture in a food processor or blender and grind the mixture finely. For additional taste, add mushrooms when sautéing the onion.

Tasty Potato Filling

This is a traditional pierogi filling. It can be a main dish served with a salad or soup or it can be a tasty side dish served with any meat or fish that you would normally complete with a rice, noodles or potatoes dish.

Ingredients
- 5 lbs. potatoes
- salt and pepper to taste
- 1/4 lb. cream cheese
- 1/4 softened butter
- 1 lb. Farmer's cheese (dry cottage cheese can be used as a substitute)

Directions

Peel the potatoes and cut them in half or quarters. In a large pot, boil the potatoes until soft. Drain the potatoes. While the potatoes are still hot, add the cream cheese, butter and Farmer's cheese. Blend well. Allow filling to cool before spooning it into the dough.

Spicy Potato and Onion Filling

Ingredients
- 3 medium baking potatoes (about 1 1/2 lb.), peeled and cut into 1-inch slices
- 2 tbs. unsalted butter
- 1tbs. vegetable oil
- 1 small onion, chopped
- 1 clove garlic, finely minced
- 1/2 tsp. dried thyme
- 2 cups finely shredded white cabbage
- 2 tbs. freshly grated Parmesan cheese
- 1 tsp. chopped fresh parsley

Directions
In a large pot, place the potatoes in a pot and cover with water. Add a dash of salt. Boil until soft (about 15 minutes).

Melt the butter and the oil together in a large sauté pan over medium heat. To this mixture add the onion, garlic, and thyme. Cook this mixture about 3 minutes on low heat. Add the cabbage and cook on medium heat for about 10 minutes, stirring occasionally. Simmer until the cabbage and onion become soft, for about 20 minutes more. Add salt and pepper.

Drain the potatoes when they are soft. Add the cabbage mixture, the cheese, and the parsley. Mash this mixture until it is well blended with no potato lumps. Add a dash of salt and pepper. Make sure the filling is cool before spooning it onto the dough.

Original Cheese Filling

Ingredients
- 1 1/2 cups cottage cheese (drained)
- 1/4 tsp. vanilla
- 1 egg yolk
- 1 tbsp. butter (melted)
- 1/2 tsp. salt
- 1 1/2 tbsp. sugar

Directions
Drain the cottage cheese and place in a medium sized bowl. Combine the rest of the ingredients and mix until smooth.

Easy Cheese and Potato Filling

This filling is firmer than either cheese or potato alone. The combination of the flavors is delicious. We have these pierogi often as a side dish with fish and chicken.

Ingredients
- 1 cup dry cottage cheese
- 1 cup whipped potatoes
- 1 tbsp. onions (chopped fine)
- salt and pepper to taste

Directions
In a large bowl, combine the ingredients and mix lightly. Spoon filling on to the dough.

Cheddar Cheese and Potato Filling

Ingredients

- 6-8 medium potatoes, peeled and cut in half
- 1 cup grated cheddar cheese
- 1/2 cup finely chopped onion
- 2 tablespoons oil

Directions

Sauté the onion in the oil on low heat. Cook and mash the potatoes. To the mashed potatoes add the sautéed onions and the grated cheddar cheese. Mix well.

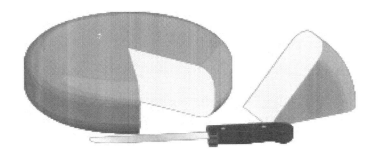

Sweet Cheese Filling

Ingredients
- 1 lb. Farmer's Cheese
- 1/4 cup sugar
- 1 egg and 1 egg yolk
- 1/2 tsp. vanilla extract
- 3/4 teaspoon cinnamon (optional)

Directions
Mix all ingredients together by hand. For a tasty variation, add cinnamon.

Marvelous Prune Filling

Ingredients
- 20 prunes with pits
- 1 tablespoon sugar
- 1 teaspoon lemon juice
- 3/4 tsp. cinnamon
- 1/2 teaspoon ground cloves

Directions
Place prunes in saucepan and cover them with water. Bring to a boil. Turn off the heat. Add the sugar, lemon juice, cinnamon and cloves. Cover. Let steep 15-20 minutes. When cool, drain and remove pits from prunes. Refrigerate until ready to use.

Putting It All Together

If you have never made pierogies before, this part may be a little intimidating. Your first ones may not look picture perfect, but they will taste great! And in no time, you will be making pierogies that you will be proud to serve to your fussiest of guests.

I will do my best to describe the process below. However if you are a visual person, I suggest that you search on YouTube for a video on how to make pierogies. There are dozen of videos that are quite helpful.

1. For potato filling or potato/cheese filling, you can spread the filling on the cut-out dough. For all other fillings put about 1 to 2 teaspoons of the filling in the center of the dough. Leave about 1/4 inch around the edge so that it will close easily.

2. Fold the dough over the filling so that edges meet.

3. Holding the pierogi in one hand, with your other hand, take your thumb and first finger and press evenly around the edge. Start at one end and press together. Move your thumb and finger down a smidge and press again. Continue to do this until the end of the rim.

Cooking the Pierogies

All pierogies should be boiled before frying. For heavier fillings, like potato and potato/cheese, freeze the pierogies overnight before boiling. By doing this, the pierogi will be less likely to break apart when boiling.

To keep the pierogies from sticking to each other, place a teaspoon of oil into the water. Bring the water to a boil and then lower the heat to medium-low. Place the pierogi on a large spoon and drop it gently into the boiling water. Do not over-crowd the pierogies. When the pierogies begin to float, take them out, one at a time with a large spoon and place them on a plate to cool and dry. Take extra caution to not come in direct contact with the hot water.

Once the pierogies have been boiled, they can be fried in butter and eaten right away. If you do not plan on eating all of the pierogies right away, refrigerate or freeze the pierogies after boiling.

When you are ready to eat the pierogies, fry them SLOWLY, on low heat, in a pan with 1 to 2 tablespoons of butter. The pierogies will get golden brown. Do not rush this procedure. The best flavors come forth when they are browned slowly.

Pierogi Casseroles

If you do not have the time to make individual pierogies, pierogi casseroles can be just what you need. These casseroles will give you the great pierogi taste that you crave with less work.

Quick and Easy Pierogi Casserole

Ingredients
- 1 (16 oz.) pkg. frozen pierogies
- 5 large plum tomatoes
- 2 large onions
- 1 (8 oz.) pkg. mushrooms
- 3 tbsp. oil
- 1 tbsp. chopped parsley
- dash of salt and pepper

Directions
Preheat oven to 350 degrees (F). Prepare the frozen pierogies as directed on the package.

Dice the tomatoes and slice the onions and mushrooms. In a medium sized skillet place the oil, onions and mushrooms. Cook over medium heat until the mushrooms and onions are soft and golden. Add the tomatoes, parsley, salt, pepper and water to the onions and mushrooms. Heat to boiling.

Place the pierogies in a casserole dish. Pour the onion mushroom mixture on top of the pierogies. Cover the casserole dish. Bake for 30-35 minutes. Makes 4 servings.

Homemade Pierogi Casserole

Ingredients
- 5 potatoes, peeled and cut in half
- 1/2 cup milk
- 1/2 cup butter, melted
- 1/2 pound bacon, diced
- 1 onion, chopped
- 6 cloves garlic, minced
- 1/2 (16 ounce) package lasagna noodles
- 2 cups shredded Cheddar cheese
- salt and pepper to taste
- 1 (8 ounce) container sour cream
- 3 tablespoons chopped fresh chives

Directions
Preheat oven to 350 degrees (F).

Cook the lasagna noodles as per the directions on the package. When cooked, cool them under cool running water and drain. Set the noodles aside.

In a large pot with water, place the potatoes. Bring to a boil and continue to cook until the potatoes are soft. Remove from the heat and drain. Place the milk and 6 tablespoons of melted butter in with the potatoes and mash. Set the potatoes aside.

Place the 2 remaining tablespoons of butter in a large skillet. Sauté the bacon, onion and garlic over medium heat. Continue to cook for 5 minutes.

Layer the following ingredients in a 9 x 13 inch baking dish:

- Half of the mashed potatoes on the bottom.
- Next place 1/3 of the cheese.
- Next place a layer of lasagna noodles.

36

- Next place the remaining potatoes, another 1/3 of the cheese and another layer of noodles.
- Place the bacon, onion and garlic over the noodles, then another layer of noodles.
- Top with the remaining cheese.
- Add salt and pepper to taste.

Place uncovered dish in the oven, and bake at 350 degrees (F) for 30 to 45 minutes. Serve with sour cream and chopped fresh chives.

Makes 6 to 8 servings.

Final Thoughts

When making several batches of pierogies at one time, you may want to freeze some for a later date. To do this, boil them first. Make sure the pierogies are completely dry before placing them in an airtight container or ziplock bag. Frozen pierogies are best eaten within two to three weeks. Defrost the pierogies before frying to ensure even and thorough cooking.

Pierogies not eaten and not frozen should be placed in an airtight container and placed in the refrigerator. In the refrigerator they will keep 3 to 4 days.

Making pierogies is an excellent way to bring family together. Make them with your children and grandchildren and pass down this wonderful treat. Experiment with different fillings and create your own family recipes and traditions.

If you enjoyed this book, please pick up a copy of my FREE mini-cookbook:

Healthy Changes to Famous Desserts

http://tinyurl.com/HealthyDesserts

Wishing you happy creating, cooking and eating!

~ Kathy

Made in the USA
Lexington, KY
11 December 2012